Smelly Science

Messy Medicine

Dr Mary Dobson

Illustrated by Vince Reid

OXFORD
UNIVERSITY PRESS

Oxford University Press, Great Clarendon Street, Oxford OX2 6DP

Oxford New York

Athens Auckland Bangkok Bogotá Buenos Aires Calcutta
Cape Town Chennai Dar es Salaam Delhi Florence Hong Kong Istanbul
Karachi Kuala Lumpur Madrid Melbourne Mexico City Mumbai
Nairobi Paris São Paulo Singapore Taipei Tokyo Toronto Warsaw
and associated companies in Berlin Ibadan

Oxford is a registered trade mark of Oxford University Press

Cover artwork by Vince Reid.
Photographs reproduced by kind permission of: p22 Mehau Kulyk/SPL;
p8 Barry Dowsett/SPL; p10 David Scharf/SPL; p18 Science and Society Picture
Library; p15 Wellcome Institute Library
SPL = Science Photo Library

British Library Cataloguing in Publication Data
available

ISBN 0 19 910574 X

1 3 5 7 9 10 8 6 4 2

Printed in Great Britain

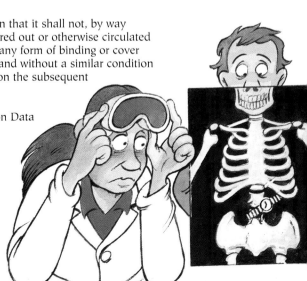

Contents

Scratch and sniff the scented panels lightly with a fingernail
to release their smell.

Science Makes Sense

Have you ever had a stinking cold and wondered why your friends won't come near you? Or felt (and smelled) so rotten that even the doctor had to put on a mask before prodding you? Remember the last time someone threw up after a school lunch? There are heaps of rotten reasons for feeling lousy, so poke your nose into *Messy Medicine* for a real sense of medical science.

Science explains the world around you — both what you can see and what is hidden, the living and the non-living. It's a wonderful mix of facts, figures, experiments and observations — science can be fun! And, as you're about to find out, it can also be smelly!

Sick!
A nasty disease called cholera produces vile vomit, reeking runs and can turn its victims black, blue and green.

In the past, many people thought that bad smells caused disease - not such a silly idea, really. One whiff of a pile of stinky horse poo or an overflowing toilet was enough to make you feel pretty queasy. Fortunately, by the 1860s scientists had begun to sniff out the truth — grisly germs were discovered, and great germbusters were invented to clean up the rot.

Ancient aromatic therapy
The young always think they nose best. Scientists today have discovered that sweet wormwood — a plant we used thousands of years ago to get rid of worms — can cure malaria.

The amazing (and disgusting) discoveries made in medicine in the 20th century would turn our ancestors green with envy. But the ancients would also laugh if they knew that some of their mouldy medicines are now being revived.

Messy Medicine takes you straight to the heart of the matter. It's full of the pongs of pus, puke and pee. There are rotten reminders of mouldy medicines and loathsome leeches, as well as oozing operations and pungent pills for all kinds of deadly diseases. So scratch and sniff for some mouldy whiffs. But don't worry — you won't catch anything from the foul smells in this book! They've all been tested and approved by smelly scientists!

A spoonful of sugar

Yuck! Many medicines taste so foul they make us feel even sicker, so those crafty chemists add a spoonful of sugar to help the medicine go down.

All stitched up

This South American Indian healer uses giant black ants to seal a wound. Their jaws clamp the wound together, and the doctor cuts away their bodies, leaving the patient neatly stitched up.

Read on to find out just what makes us sick, and sample the best, and the worst, of messy medicine.

Feeling Foul?

Feeling healthy means no sign of dis-comfort or dis-ease. No aches, no pains, not a drop of snot or a squelchy spot in sight. Unfortunately, most of us feel foul some of the time. Our bodies have all sorts of ways of protesting when we do. We may just let off steam! Or break out in itchy rashes and smelly sweats. Sometimes we cough, splutter and sneeze, throw up or squat down. We get runny noses and runny tums, awful aches and pains, bumps and lumps, bloody bruises and pus-filled oozes. There are endless symptoms and danger signs.

Fortunately, most of these problems get better on their own — our brilliant bodies are designed to heal as well as squeal.

Throwing up can do your body a power of good. If you've eaten poisoned food, it's better out than in!

Stink!

Scratch!

Johnny Belcher: severe wind – No baked beans

Charlie Chilly: heavy cold – Bed and plenty of hankies

Mrs Pugwash: bad breath – Mouthwash

Some of the people in this doctor's surgery will go away empty-handed, without a drop of mouldy medicine.

Scratch and sniff for a sickly waiting-room whiff.

Dreadful Diseases

But sometimes those nasty symptoms don't go away. Over the centuries, there have been some dreadful, deadly diseases, and people have tried all sorts of revolting remedies. Take a look at these awful afflictions.

Smallpox

A virulent virus spread this one, which causes horrible sores. Queen Elizabeth I suffered from smallpox. She covered up her pock marks with lead-based paste, which eventually rotted her cheeks.

Typhoid

A beastly bacterial infection that causes diarrhoea and sickness. Prince Albert, Queen Victoria's husband, died of typhoid in 1861 after drinking foul water in Windsor Castle. His ghastly germs will find their way back into the water system . . .

Tuberculosis

Until recently, spitting was banned on buses in London to prevent the spread of stinking airborne diseases like tuberculosis, a terrible wasting disease that usually gets the lungs. It loves overcrowded, dirty places.

Ebola

This is the ebola virus. It causes one of the most vile diseases in Africa today. The victim's organs are turned to mush. Fortunately, it is very rare.

Foul Facts

- The Black Death in the middle of the 14th century killed 75 million people - nearly half the world's population. This plague is spread by fleas and is still around today.

- The influenza or 'flu epidemic of 1918-19 killed over 30 million people in six months — more than the First World War of 1914-18.

- By 1980 smallpox, one of the oldest and foulest diseases of all time, had been wiped out. Sadly new diseases, like AIDS, are spreading fast.

- In Africa, malaria is the main cause of the death of children. It kills about 2 million every year. Malaria means 'bad air', because in the old days people thought it was caused by foul smells from swamps. Now we know it is spread by mosquitoes.

- In many countries, cancer and heart disease are the biggest killers. They mostly affect older people.

A century ago, there were so many dreadful diseases, and medicine was so measly, that people could only expect to live to the age of 30. Today, messy medicines, healthy diets and keeping clean have helped control diseases and lengthen our lives in many parts of the world. The Japanese, the longest-lived population, can expect to live to the age of 80. In poor parts of Africa, however, people still cannot expect to live beyond the age of 55.

Ghastly Germs

Take a deep breath and open wide.
What ghastly germs have sneaked inside?

Many diseases are caused by ghastly germs that are so tiny they can only be seen under a microscope. Take a look under your fingernail — it may be filthy dirty or squeaky clean, but there are hundreds of invisible little bugs waiting to find a way into your body. They can't normally get through your tough, germ-proof skin — unless you have an open cut — but there are a few perfect places for them to sneak in. Think about (but don't scratch and sniff) your main openings — from top to bottom. How many germ holes have you got?

Germs also escape from these openings. A snotty sneeze can blast out a fountain of germs at about 150 km per hour. Ugh! Those germs can then be recycled — your best friend gets a whiff of your germs, and before long the whole class is down with the latest bug.

Nature has created lots of different types of germs, and they can be spread in a frightening variety of lousy ways.

BEASTLY BACTERIA

Bacteria are microscopic living cells. There are billions all around us. Not all of them are harmful, but some produce foul diseases or deadly poisons inside our bodies. A common disease caused by bacteria is gingivitis — or rotten gums. This one's not infectious, so you can't catch it from anyone else. You get it when bits of food get stuck in your gums and go horribly rotten. A few bacteria can rapidly multiply into millions. Hope you remembered to brush your teeth this morning!

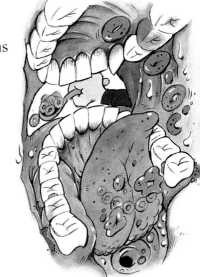

VILE VIRUSES

Viruses are even tinier than bacteria. Millions could fit on a full stop. They survive and multiply by invading living cells. The most common infectious virus is the common cold. There is no known cure. Atishoo!

BRUTAL BLOODSUCKERS

Blood-sucking creatures, like fleas, mosquitoes, and tsetse flies, can pierce your skin and inject nasty bacteria, viruses or parasites into your body with each greedy gulp of blood. Malicious mosquitoes spread malaria.

FEELING LOUSY?

Insects can also leave their droppings for you to pick up. The droppings of the dust mite can cause allergies like asthma. The poo of body lice contains a brutal bacterium, which when scratched into an open wound causes a revolting disease called typhus. Head lice can be irritating but, fortunately, they don't get under your skin.

A blood–sucking body louse

Germ Gobblers and Body Wobblers

Doctors are trained to sniff out our diseases. To help them make a diagnosis, they might take a bit of blood or a fresh specimen. Follow Ruby's case to see what's bugging her.

Ruby has a large red oozing boil on her bottom. It started as an itchy spot, which Ruby scratched until it bled. When a scab formed, she picked it off, and now it's full of yellow pus.

Doc Dougherty prods and pokes. It's a real stinker, and there's only one solution – send samples to the lab boys. It's amazing what can be spotted in a blob of blood, a pinch of pus, and a wee drop of wee.

These are their fabulous findings:

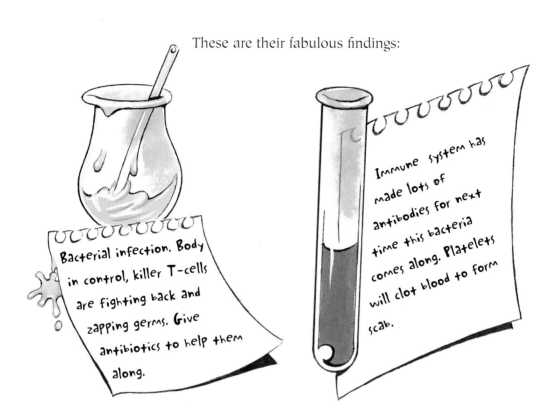

Bacterial infection. Body in control, killer T-cells are fighting back and zapping germs. Give antibiotics to help them along.

Immune system has made lots of antibodies for next time this bacteria comes along. Platelets will clot blood to form scab.

GERM OR GENE?

Ruby's body defences gobbled up the invading germs pretty well – but did she also have a disease, called diabetes, caused partly by family genes? It's our 100,000 genes that carry all the instructions on how our bodies are built and run. If one of them is faulty, we may get ill. Lucky for Ruby, the sugar in her wee was actually because she'd drunk too much cola at lunch. She's had enough of a fright to know not to keep scratching those scummy scabs!

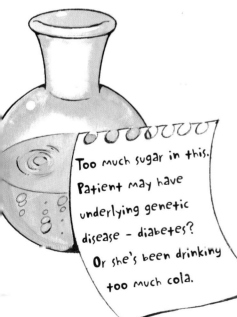

Too much sugar in this. Patient may have underlying genetic disease - diabetes? Or she's been drinking too much cola.

Mouldy Medicines

Our bodies have remarkable ways of healing. But sometimes we need extra ammunition to stop a disease getting out of control. Medicines of all kinds have been used over the centuries to cure and treat illness. Some look and taste utterly disgusting, a few are amazingly effective, while others are totally crazy. Sample this lot and see how many you can stomach!

Loathsome leeches

At one time people believed that diseases were caused by bad humours (fluids) in the body. This wasn't funny, as leeches were stuck all over their bare parts to suck out bad blood. Unfortunately, these loathsome worms actually sucked out all the good blood. Today, these bloodsucking beasts are back in fashion — they are often popped on to patients to keep the blood flowing after minor surgery.

Medicinal maggots

If our ancestors believed bad smells caused disease, they obviously thought smells could cure them too! Dung was an essential part of many old rotten remedies. Imagine having a slab of pig's poo on your cut knee. Within a few days, it might be crawling with mouldy maggots. But, believe it or not, those maggots could be doing a great job eating up all the messy, fleshy bits.

Scratch and sniff these medicinal maggots and you'll feel even more foul!

Bitter barks

Several bitter-tasting medicines from plants have remarkable powers. Aspirin, which is a general painkiller and helps control heart problems, was originally found in the bark of the willow tree.

Sickly and soft

Some medicines are specially designed to make you throw up, or soften up. Emetics give you a second taste of your lunch, and laxatives get things moving in the other direction!

A Chinese constipation roller, used to massage the stomach to get things moving!

Aspirin is now made in laboratories - and billions of tablets are sold each year.

Oils for boils

Today there are oils, creams, pills, lotions and potions for every tiny little problem. Some can be bought over the counter without a doctor's prescription.

Simple solutions

In poor countries, children suffer from terrible diarrhoea which can quickly lead to loss of body fluids and rapid death. The simple solution of salt, sugar and clean water is a remarkably effective treatment.

A mouldy miracle

A slice of mouldy bread may make you turn green, but as you'll discover on page 25, scientists discovered that this mould could save millions of lives.

Pills for all ills?

There isn't a magic pill for every ill, but turn the page for a remarkable way to stop disease in the first place - a juicy jab!

Juicy Jabs

Imagine taking pus from a large, juicy, smallpox pimple and jabbing it into someone else to prevent them dying from this deadly disease. Now imagine taking pus from a cow with cowpox (a bit like chickenpox) - and using it to wipe out smallpox from the world forever! Follow the remarkable story of vaccination, to find out how one disease prevented another.

The year is 1746 and everyone in England and America is talking about the latest medical breakthrough. All it takes is a bit of smallpox pus rubbed into a cut on the arm. Instead of a horrible full-blown version of smallpox, people inoculated in this way will just have a mild form and never catch smallpox again. Inoculation has already been used in some parts of the world for hundreds of years. The Chinese even blow the pus up people's noses!

Fifty years later, in 1796, Edward Jenner, an English country doctor, goes one better. In a smelly old cowshed, he comes across a milkmaid, Sarah Nelmes, with blisters on her hand. Sarah reckons she's caught cowpox from the cows. This doesn't make her ill, but completely protects her from smallpox.

Jenner decides to experiment — on an 8 year-old boy! He scratches James Phipps on the arm and pops in some cowpox pus. No sweat. Then comes the acid test. He infects James with smallpox pus. Phew! James survives, and doesn't even get a tiny pox.

Jenner calls his method 'vaccination', from the Latin word for cow, 'vacca'. But this isn't the end of the story! In the 1960s, 10 million people are still infected with smallpox. War is declared on the disease using a vaccination gun. The campaign is a resounding success, and in 1980 smallpox is declared a dead issue.

Can you remember your last vaccination? (Ouch!) You were being injected with a few germs, which made your body make antibodies to fight off the real disease. Today, there are lots of juicy jabs which prevent millions of children catching diseases like tetanus, diphtheria, measles, and whooping cough. The polio vaccine may also be given on a lump of sugar. Scientists hope that polio, like smallpox, will soon be wiped out. Meanwhile, the race is on to find more vaccines to stop the spread of other foul diseases.

Oozing Operations

Whentthe body can't cope, and medicines don't work, there's nothing else for it but the drastic solution — the surgeon's knife. This is the messiest bit of medicine, when a rotten part of the body needs cutting out or sawing off. For centuries, this was a really grisly experience and your chances of survival were thin.

This child is having his appendix removed at a boarding school in the early 19th century. Amid the stench of school lunch, the doctor carves a large slice of flesh from the boy's tum and removes an oozing appendix. There's not much he can do to stop the pain, or the blood.

Scratch and sniff the poor patient for a poisonous pong.

Today, the surgeon's tools don't look so very different, but operating theatres are usually sparkling clean and, thanks to some smelly discoveries of the late 19th century (see page 24), the patient won't feel a thing. One of the most up-to-date forms of surgery is keyhole surgery. The surgeon makes just a tiny, keyhole-sized cut in the patient and pokes in some powerful little tools.

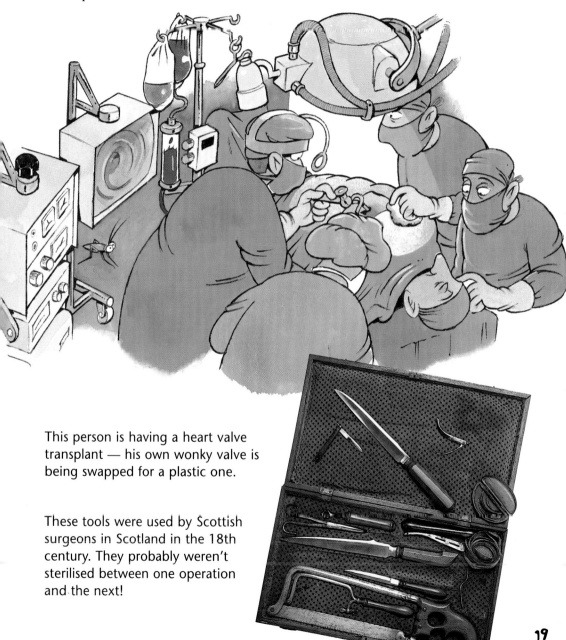

This person is having a heart valve transplant — his own wonky valve is being swapped for a plastic one.

These tools were used by Scottish surgeons in Scotland in the 18th century. They probably weren't sterilised between one operation and the next!

Hospital Stinks

Whether it's for an oozing operation or a spot of special treatment, sometimes sick people are whipped off to hospital. Going into hospital can be quite an ordeal. The surroundings are strange, and so are the smells. Drop in on these two hospitals — they smell quite different!

Modern medicine at its best — a brand new hospital, which smells strongly of antiseptics and air fresheners. There are, however, alarming reports that not all the bugs are being beaten by smelly science.

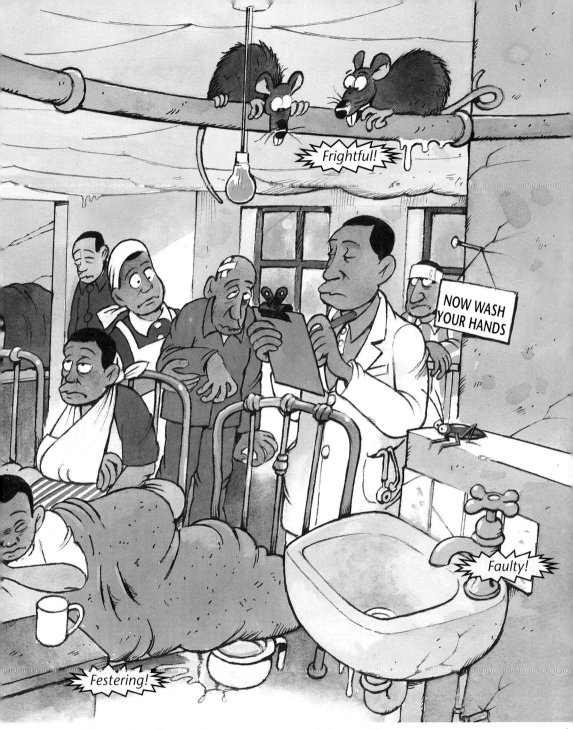

A rural hospital in the tropics. In some parts of the world, conditions in hospitals are still very poor and smelly. Doctors and nurses have to work with limited equipment and medicines.

Deadly Dissections

The human body is a mind-boggling maze of blood, muscle and bone. Have you ever wondered how doctors know all about our messy insides? In ancient times, it was dead easy! There were so many cut-up corpses lying around on the battlefield, doctors had a field day poking around in their putrefying remains. The ancient Egyptians were especially clued up. When they made their mummies, they removed all the bits that might go rotten — like the guts, brain and heart — so they really got to grips with the inside of the human body.

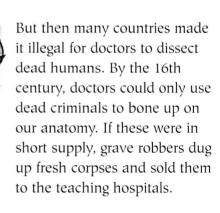

But then many countries made it illegal for doctors to dissect dead humans. By the 16th century, doctors could only use dead criminals to bone up on our anatomy. If these were in short supply, grave robbers dug up fresh corpses and sold them to the teaching hospitals.

Today, doctors are trained to know the body inside out. Learning to be a doctor can take up to seven years of blood, sweat and tears. But at least by the end of it, most doctors know every nook and cranny of our private parts.

There are also some spectacular machines to view the body in all its gory glory. X-rays, scanners and giant magnets save doctors the mess – and us the pain – of poking around our insides.

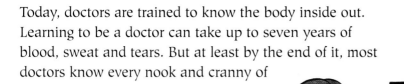

Some people leave their bodies to scientists, in case they can be useful. Some even hope that in years to come they'll be able to bring them back from the dead.

The bare and brutal truth. This amazing invention of 1895, known as an X-ray machine, gives doctors the power to see through their grisly patients!

An ultrasound scanner can see this unborn baby wrapped up in his own little world - bet you never knew your mum saw what you were up to even before you were born!

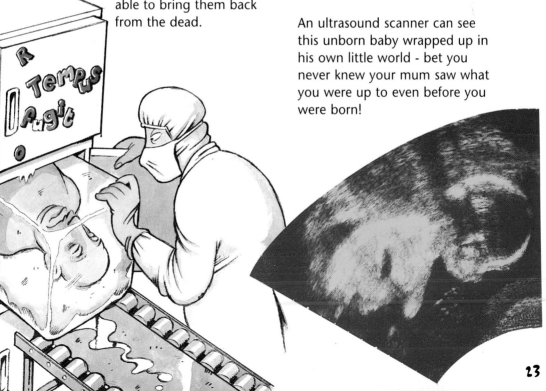

Disgusting Discoveries

Scientists sweat and toil in stinky laboratories full of ghastly gases and putrid poisons, setting up experiments to find the causes of, and cures for, diseases. Their work can be really gripping: imagine holding your breath waiting to see if an experiment has worked – and holding your nose when you discover the disgusting truth! Here are some of the most famous — and mouldy — medical discoveries of all time.

Wine exposed to air goes sour. A lump of flesh goes rotten. Decay is caused by deadly bacteria.

A Funny Smell — 1847

In some hilarious experiments, Horace Wells, William Morton and Dr James Simpson have found that funny-smelling anaesthetics like laughing gas, ether and chloroform are powerful ways of knocking out their patients. This should soon put a stop to their agonising screams in the operating theatre.

Rotten Results – 1861

The French scientist, Louis Pasteur, has made a rotten discovery. He has found that our air is full of nasty germs which can make things go rotten — including us!

These doctors nearly died of laughter trying out the new anaesthetic.

A Smelly Success – 1869

Joseph Lister, a British surgeon, has found a smelly solution – in the sewers! – to stop his patients dying like flies. A pungent chemical called carbolic acid, used to clean the sewers, has proved a great antiseptic for killing germs and stopping infection.

Miracle Mould — 1942

The most amazing medical cure of all times is just a nasty bit of old mould. Penicillin, first discovered in a dirty dish by Alexander Fleming in 1928, is now proving a miracle drug. With thousands dying in the War, Howard Florey and Ernst Chain, two Oxford scientists, are desperately trying to grow the rotten stuff in bed-pans, milk churns and biscuit tins. There is even hope that more mouldy antibiotics will be found in our stinking sewers.

Foul Fumes — 1950

Smoking causes lung cancer. This is the foul finding of a very large medical survey of doctors and their smoking habits. Some people were fuming when they heard the results.

Mad Cows and Englishmen — 1996

Everyone's hopping mad — the government has just revealed that the English may have been eating beef infected with BSE, or mad cow disease. Brainy scientists are now trying to unravel the whole truth.

A Messy Business

Doctors, dentists, nurses, healers and public health officials do a wonderful job saving lives, caring for the sick and poking their nose into other people's business. Medicine may be messy, but it's also richly rewarding.

SMELLS SUSPICIOUS

Galen (AD130-200) was a famous Roman doctor who patched up gladiators. Like many ancients, he also got reeking rich sniffing out the odd disease or two.

Dr Foulweather is a urinary specialist in a large modern hospital. He carries on the ancient tradition of examining a patient's wee for signs of disease.

MUCKY AND MAGICAL

Mr Smellie was a famous 18th-century man-midwife. No kidding! He taught his pupils how to pull babies out of their mummies' tummies.

This African woman has just helped to produce the magical event of birth. After she cuts the cord that joins the baby's tum to the mum, she will rub dung into the baby's belly button.

LOUSY LADIES

Miss Prim is a school nit-nurse. She has a really lousy job but plenty of business. There are lots of tickly heads in this school and, so far, Miss Prim has only just scratched the surface.

Florence Nightingale and Mary Seacole were 19th-century nurses who helped to mop up the appalling stinks in Scutari Hospital during the Crimean War (1854-56). The death rate dropped dramatically after their fragrant efforts.

YUCKY YANKY

Samuel Sawbones was the 17th-century equivalent to a modern dentist — he spent his life yanking teeth out of yucky mouths. At least he was lucky — sugar was becoming popular in America, and it sure was a perfect way to start the rot and bring the customers rolling in.

PUNGENT POTIONS

The 17th-century quack doctor, Robert Talbor, made a small fortune with his pungent potions. He cured putrid peasants and reeking royals in Europe of many diseases, including malaria.

Today healers, like this barefoot doctor in China, still use many valuable ancient herbal remedies.

Scratch and sniff this Chinese doctor's herbs for a healthy whiff.

Aromatic Alternatives

Medicine in the 20th century has moved forward in leaps and bounds. In some parts of the world there are great high-tech hospitals with state-of-the-art equipment and wonder drugs for nasty bugs. Highly-skilled doctors patch us up, pull us round, and put us back on our feet. But modern medicine can't provide answers for every ill, and some people use aromatic alternatives. Take your pick:

A PUNGENT PRICK

Aromatherapy and acupuncture have been used in China for over 3000 years. These deliciously smelly and soothing solutions are now popular for all sorts of problems. Americans spend $500 million a year on acupuncture.

Barbara's back feels bad, so she's inhaling the wonderful aromas of burning incense while the acupuncturist sticks fine needles into parts of her body. The effects are quite sensational.

HEAVENLY HOMEOPATHY

Homeopathic remedies use a tiny bit of an ingredient that in large doses would give you the symptoms you want cured – some people find it wonderfully effective.

A MOULDY MASSAGE

This chap has lost his sense of smell. His own medical doctor has no smelly suggestions, so he tries a spot of reflexology. The reflexologist massages his feet – and waits with baited breath to see if his patient can smell again.

A FRESH START

Today, as in the past, many people can't afford fancy medical care, but there is one great aromatic alternative to medicine: keeping clean! Some of our ancient ancestors knew it was essential to get rid of all their waste products and foul stinks. In India in 2500 BC there were baths, lavatories and proper drains. And the Romans and Greeks were also pretty fresh and clean.

This water stinks like a blocked toilet. It is used by animals and people for all their basic needs. It is seething with germs and nasty worms, which will go in people one end and come out the other.

New flushing toilets and running water are transforming life for these villagers. Keeping clean will be a great way to prevent the rot and stop the spread of germs.

In the 20th century, flushing toilets, pure drinking water and washing have been vital in helping to save lives. Sadly, in many poverty-stricken parts of the world today, the conditions of hygiene are appalling. A staggering number of diseases are carried by water, and 25 million people die each year because they do not have clean water and sanitation. Scientists at the World Health Organization are working hard to improve the health of the world's population for the 21st century.

Pungent Puzzles

SQUIRMY, WORMY AND GERMY

If you've had the guts to scratch and sniff your way through *Messy Medicine*, you will have discovered that bugs love rubbish, toilets, dung heaps, dirty water, muck, manure, rotten food — anything that stinks — and that includes YOU!

This squirmy tapeworm is trying to find a smelly spot for a spicy little snack. Tapeworms can be up to 9 metres long and can do horrible things to our insides. See if you can arrange these pictures into the correct order, to follow the route of the worm and find out where it will end up! What is the best way to stop this mess?

AWFUL ANAGRAMS

Rearrange these letters to make:

a mouldy medicine which has saved millions of lives

C L L I I I N N P E

a runny tummy

O A A R R H E D I

a wonderfully smelly treatment using aromatic oils

T R R A A A P M O Y H E

Glossary

acupuncture a traditional Chinese medical practice, using fine needles inserted through the skin to cure illness and relieve pain.

allergy a reaction of the body to certain substances such as dust, pollen or some foods.

anaesthetics drugs used to stop you feeling pain.

antibiotics medicines, such as penicillin, that are used to treat bacterial diseases. They are usually made by bacteria or fungi.

antibodies substances in the blood which protect the body by fighting germs.

antiseptics substances used to destroy germs.

aromatherapy therapy using massage and aromatic oils.

bacteria microscopic single-celled forms of life, some of which can cause disease.

constipation difficulty in opening the bowels.

emetics medicines which make you vomit.

genes the parts of the DNA in our cells which carry information about our bodies.

germ a microbe that can cause disease.

homeopathy a form of medical treatment in which tiny amounts of substances are given which in large amounts would produce symptoms of the disease.

immune system a collection of cells and organs in the body that work together to fight infections.

keyhole surgery surgery where only a small cut is made into the body.

laxatives medicines which help to loosen the bowels.

midwife someone who is trained to help in childbirth.

parasite a small living thing that may live on the skin or inside the body. Lice and tapeworms are parasites.

transplant a technique in surgery to transfer tissue or an organ from one body, or part of a body, to another.

vaccination a way of making people immune to a disease.

virus a very small infectious particle which can invade and take over living cells, causing disease.

Index